SEPARATION rev. ed.

Supporting Children in Their Preschool Transitions

Kathe Jervis and Barbara K. Polland

National Association for the Education of Young Children
Washington, DC

National Association for the Education of Young Children
1313 L Street NW, Suite 500
Washington, DC 20005-4101
202-232-8777 or 800-424-2460
www.naeyc.org

Separation: Supporting Children in Their Preschool Transitions

Through its publications program the National Association for the Education of Young Children (NAEYC) provides a forum for discussion of major issues and ideas in the early childhood field, with the hope of provoking thought and promoting professional growth. The views expressed or implied in this book are not necessarily those of the Association.

Carol Copple, *publications director*; Bry Pollack, *managing editor*; Malini Dominey, *design and production*; Cassandra Berman, *editorial associate*; Melissa Edwards, *editorial assistant*; Natalie Klein Cavanagh, *photo editor*; Sandi Collins, *front cover design*

Library of Congress Control Number: 2007932128
ISBN: 978-1-928896-44-9
NAEYC Item #230

About the Authors

For more than 25 years, **Kathe Jervis** taught K–12 and college courses in Massachusetts, California, and New York. She has written about children and classrooms in *Harvard Educational Review, Educational Leadership,* and *Phi Delta Kappan.* While a Senior Research Associate at the National Center for Restructuring Education, Schools, and Teaching (NCREST) at Teachers College, Columbia University, she wrote *Eyes on the Child: Three Portfolio Stories* (Teachers College Press, 1996). She participates in national educational communities such as the Prospect Center for Education and Research and the North Dakota Study Group on Evaluation.

Barbara K. Polland is Professor of Child and Adolescent Development at California State University, Northridge; a psychotherapist in private practice; and the author of books for parents, teachers, and children. She has worked professionally with children for 50 years, but says her own son and daughter "have been my best teachers." She has shared her approaches to early care on radio and television, in magazine and newspaper articles, and in conference presentations and seminars in the United States, Mexico, and Japan. She is the author of *No Directions on the Package: A Practical Guide for Parents with Children from Birth to Age 12* (Celestial Arts, 2000) and *We Can Work It Out: Conflict Resolution for Children* (Tricycle Press, 2000).

To our grandchildren, Daniel, Joshua, and Sadie, and to children everywhere who are taking the journey toward independence with the support of their families and teachers.

We met as friends and colleagues when our own children began the process of separation. We've shared the joys and trials of parenting long enough to see our children have children of their own. Having a candid friend to discuss the minute details of parenting and exchange stories of our children's growth has been an anchor in our professional and personal lives.

Contents

Acknowledgments

With appreciation to Jean Berlfein and her family for sponsoring the 1984 conference on Attachment, Separation, and Loss in memory of her mother, Edna Reiss. Their commitment to children and to Bowlby's work has served as an inspiration for this 2007 publication. We would also like to extend our appreciation to the dedicated early childhood teachers and the parents who have the challenge of helping children to successfully begin school.

How This Publication Came to Be

In September 1984, her family and the Reiss-Davis Child Study Center of Los Angeles hosted a conference to honor the memory of Edna Reiss, an early advocate for the mental health of children. That conference, *Attachment, Separation, and Loss: Impact on Pre-School Child Care,* was a scholarly and practical exploration of children's transitions from home to their first early childhood settings. It was attended by researchers and practitioners, as well as parents of young children. The proceedings of that conference became the book *Separation: Strategies for Helping Two- to Four-Year-Olds*, edited by Kathe Jervis and published by NAEYC since 1987.

In 2007, NAEYC invited Kathe Jervis, the initial documenter of the conference, and Barbara Polland, a conference participant and contributor to the original publication, to update the book. The Association thanks them both for the time and effort they donated to this project as a contribution to the profession they love.

—Eds.

Introduction

A major developmental task for a young child is becoming independent in the world. The process of separation—leaving family and familiar surroundings, trusting they will be there to return to, reconnecting, then venturing out again—figures prominently.

A child's first entry into preschool or child care is a major separation event. Some children quickly settle in, accept friendly overtures, and show interest in their new surroundings. Others have difficulty. They may protest, cry, cling, or act sad and withdrawn when faced with new settings and unfamiliar adults. No one sees and feels the effects of these behaviors and emotions more than children's families and teachers.[1] What can we do to ease these naturally stressful transitions?

A teacher can never know any child as the family does. Teachers need help from families to understand children's temperaments and backgrounds so that both family and teacher can begin to understand each child's individual response to separation. Sharing the care and education of a child is truly a joint venture between family and teacher, never more so than in that first handover from parent to "stranger." The very nature of the handover requires families and teachers to stand together—sometimes quite literally. For that reason, we address this book to all the adults who help young children master the transitions of separation—to fathers, mothers, foster parents, grandparents, extended family members, and legal guardians, as well as early childhood teachers in centers and schools, family child care providers, all-day caregivers, program directors, and play group leaders.

Our goal is twofold: first, to help teachers and families understand separation; and second, to help them think through the policy and practice implications that follow from that understanding.

We present stories from and strategies for both home and classroom, so that families and teachers can consider not only their own roles but each other's, too. Parents meet challenges for their individual children; teachers face dilemmas that arise out of group life in classrooms. Many families handle separation smoothly without ever having heard the term; others could use some help. The more that families and teachers understand each other and the more they work together, the better off children will be.

While it's a given that parents are the most important adults in their children's lives, competent, caring, well-trained early childhood teachers have an absolutely crucial role. But within a team approach, we believe that it is the teacher who should take the lead in structuring children's separation transitions.

Finally, because this book is so focused on helping children cope with the stress and anxieties of separation around starting preschool, it is easy to forget how much children can enjoy themselves there. They take pleasure in seeing their friends. They relish having a place of their own where they can enlarge their circle of trusted adults. And they grow and learn to feel safe and independent in another environment.

Separation anxieties, so magnified here, are a natural and typically manageable bump in the road in young children's developing of autonomy and independence, in their joining of the larger world beyond their home. It can seem hard to believe, especially about a tearful 3-year-old who spends the first hour clinging to her parent's leg. But eventually children do prefer to join in to make clay snakes, swing high above the playground, listen to *Where the Wild Things Are,* build blocks with friends, and slosh at the water table.

It's understandable if teachers and families, in the midst of a child's separation struggles, momentarily forget the pleasure to be found in young children's company, in their responsiveness, humor, curiosity, and increasing maturity. If even just a few among a new group of 3-, 4-, or 5-year-olds are distraught, it's easy to feel overwhelmed and frustrated. But coming to the situation informed and prepared with effective strategies lets teachers and families relax a bit to work together in helping children successfully adjust, cope, and grow.

When young children master first separations—among many separations to come—they are on their way to becoming secure, independent people, who feel free to explore, to discover, and to learn. Our role, as the important adults in children's lives, is to support and celebrate their mastery of this developmental challenge of early childhood. As much as anything else we do, that matters.

---

1. For simplicity, when we refer to "parents" or "families," we mean anyone playing the familial role in the child's life. Similarly, when we refer to "teachers," we mean any adult responsible for children in any of the variety of early childhood care and education settings, particularly preschool.

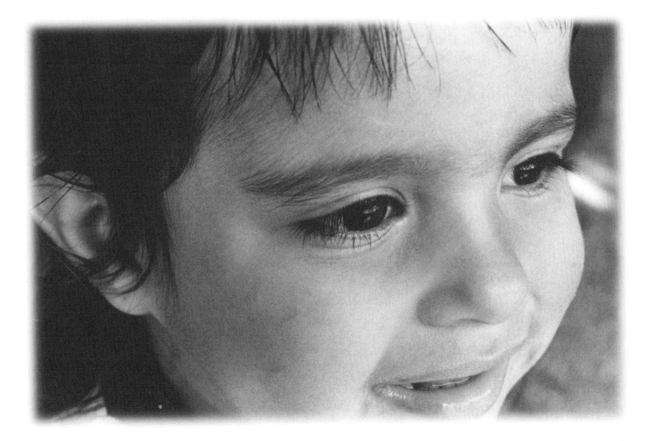

1

Attachment Theory and Preschool Separations

Separation anxiety is a universal phenomenon. In the 1982 movie *E.T.: The Extra-Terrestrial*, a small, cuddly alien crash-lands on Earth. He is stranded in a world of unfamiliar sights, sounds, and customs. No matter how well his new human friends care for him, he still yearns for his own planet. He makes initially panicked, increasingly despairing—but in the movie, ultimately successful—attempts to "phone home" for rescue. E.T.'s reactions are not unlike the separation reactions of some children making a preschool transition.

Starting preschool (or any big change in care) is a major childhood event. Understandably, most children approach the strange, new setting a little shy or anxious. Some embrace the new experience with confidence and enthusiasm. But others, especially children new to group care, loudly insist on going home. Like E.T., some become frantic or despairing. Some others cry or cling, or even kick or bite. The distressed behavior may last only a few minutes. But sometimes it can go on for days or weeks. It might not appear immediately. It might come and go for no apparent reason.

A young child's response to separation can be confusing and painful to watch for family and teacher. Understanding where the response might be coming from can help everyone respond in developmentally appropriate ways.

Attachment theory

In his seminal books *Attachment* (1969) and *Separation* (1973), British psychoanalyst John Bowlby (1907–1990) formulated what is now a foundational theory of child development: To grow up mentally healthy, a young child must have a "warm, intimate, and continuous relationship" with the mother (or "permanent mother-substitute") that gives "satisfaction and enjoyment" to both mother and child (1969, 13). A strong, positive emotional bond is necessary and good.

It seems so obvious to us now. But when he first suggested it in the 1950s, Bowlby's theory challenged what many psychologists, child care practitioners, and parents believed: That it was enough to meet only a child's physical needs. That a child's distress at being apart from the mother was the result of having been "spoiled by too much attention"—something to be avoided in child rearing.

By carefully observing young children, Bowlby also concluded that this strong bond, or *attachment*, develops over time from the interactions between child and adult (the "attachment figure"). And that the bond has a biological basis. An infant's "attachment behaviors," such as crying, smiling, following, and clinging, are innate. They evolved to make adult humans *want* to care for and protect infants of the species. Bowlby also suggested that psychological problems later in life result from attachment that was dysfunctional or missing in childhood.

Other researchers have built on and modified his ideas and added new ones of their own. In particular, his colleague Mary Ainsworth (1913–1999) added the idea of *secure* and *insecure* attachment. A child with a secure attachment to his attachment figure interacts positively and openly with her. He becomes visibly upset when she leaves and is happy to see her when she comes back. She reliably responds in an attentive, caring way to his needs, which builds his sense of security in the world. That secure feeling gives the child confidence to explore new things and settings, knowing he has her safe base to return to. When he is tired or afraid or hurt, he seeks her out for comfort. (For more, and a discussion of *insecure* attachment, see Honig 2002.)

Parents are not the only source of attachment figures for children. Bowlby's "permanent mother-substitutes" can also be other family members, neighbors, guardians—any adult who acts as a child's primary caregiver. Moreover, we know that children can form healthy attachments to more than one such adult at a time. Continued exposure to predictable caregivers enables children to create new bonds. Teachers can help a young child adapt to new surroundings, and may become the child's attachment figures themselves. Just as parents develop bonds with their children over time, teachers can too.

All humans crave a sense of security. We need a base from which we can move out into the world and to which we can return when the going gets tough. A secure attachment in infancy and early childhood is the foundation for bonding successfully with others throughout life. When a child has never formed such an attachment, forging new relationships, especially positive ones, is far more difficult. Building children's secure attachments is so important that it should be a "prime goal" of family and teacher, as it is the "keystone for ensuring children's sound mental health" (Honig 1993).

In his attachment work, Bowlby paid less attention to children's individual personality traits, such as *easygoing, difficult, feisty, flexible, intense, demanding, slow-to-warm, cautious, calm.* Now we know that personality style also plays a role in how children react to separation. Some reactions may have nothing to do with attachment and everything to do with temperament (Honig 2002). This makes temperament another psychological factor that family and teacher must understand and account for in easing children's separation transitions.

Understanding separation reactions

It might seem hard to see how a child's clinging or silent sobbing or sitting listlessly on the sidelines or determined resistance is in any way positive. Parents and teachers often want to divert the crying in particular, because it feels so impossible to deal with the tears. They often can have the impression that something is "wrong" with the child who clings, or the mother who wants to stay at school, or the teacher who feels an extra tug as a certain child goes home at the end of the day. However, all these behaviors at separation show there is an attachment between child and adult.

Attachment theory explains why children who have formed healthy attachments to an attachment figure instinctively respond with anxiety, sadness, or anger to an unwanted separation, or even a *threat* of separation, from that person. Illness, fatigue, hunger, or strange situations intensify these reactions, especially for children, as does the child's individual temperament. Attachment theory also offers an explanation for why the attachment figure—parent or teacher—might have these same feelings and impulses.

Separation and attachment are natural parts of the human cycle. Most children learn to deal with the anxiety surrounding a separation as they become increasingly autonomous, but separation issues are lifelong. Children and their parents—maybe parents even more—naturally have qualms about embarking on the sometimes rocky path toward independence from each other.

Teachers can contribute to a family's well-being by helping parents and children navigate transitions between family circle and preschool (or other child care setting) with a minimum of stress. Both parents and teachers will be more effective if they are aware of alternative ways to think about and deal with separation: hence this compendium of stories and strategies for all who are concerned with the mental health of young children.

2

Starting at Home

The transition to preschool (or other care setting) begins at home. If we are to help children become autonomous, we all need to recognize and accept the strong emotions that separation engenders. Parents and teachers need to pay attention to the behavioral details surrounding such transitions, details often overlooked in the daily shuffle of events.

Although the following account may seem extreme, it shows how strong feelings can emerge at the prospect of separation and change. Morning routines can be affected by children's feelings about separation. In turn, the way families handle such situations can affect children's behavior in the classroom. Families and teachers must find ways to make separation as smooth as possible, starting with the daily leaving home.

> After her alarm goes off, Peter's mom rushes to wake him up for his third day of preschool, saying briskly, "Time to get up. We have to get you to school."

"I don't want to get up," Peter says and pulls the covers up over his head.

She tells him, "Get dressed," and runs off to prepare breakfast. But in five minutes she hears loud wailing. She finds Peter in the bathroom; tears are streaming down his face. "What's the matter?" she asks.

"My blue shirt!" He is just standing there, looking at his shirt floating in the toilet.

"How did your shirt get into the toilet?" Annoyed, his mother points to a stack of clean laundry. "Fine. You can wear one of these."

Peter continues to cry. "Don't want them. Want my blue one."

"But it's wet and dirty. We can't get it clean before school." She fishes out the shirt, throws it into the sink, and hands him one from the stack. "How about this one?" Peter refuses as she offers him several others. Finally, she gets him dressed. She suspects the shirt "fell" into the toilet so Peter could delay going to preschool. "But I don't have time to deal with that now," she thinks.

By raising her voice, she gets Peter to sit down at the breakfast table. He is not wearing the shirt he wants and is still sniffling. Peter's mother eats with him, but the food sits in her stomach like lead. Finally it's time to go. She grabs her keys, but as she slams the front door, Peter shrieks. "What now?" she demands.

"Kiss Beboo bye-bye!" Peter has a number of rituals, and kissing his favorite stuffed animal good-bye before leaving the house is one. She grudgingly unlocks the door, and they go through the house. But they can't find the teddy bear. Peter is truly heartbroken, but at this point Peter's mom is shaking with frustration—she's going to be late for her dentist appointment, and he's late for preschool. "Look, we've got to go." She maneuvers him to the car and into his car seat.

Finally they arrive at Peter's preschool. He is clinging to his mother, his tears staining her favorite blue pants. She pries him loose, passing him to the waiting teacher. Peter is still whimpering as she turns to go, her own emotions torn between relief and guilt.

How could Peter's mom have created a calmer climate for them both? If she had thought more about *why* mornings were so stressful, and realized how stress makes separation so much harder for children, she may have reacted differently. What strategies might have worked better in this specific situation?

What about the shirt?

Peter's mother had made all the decisions herself that morning. She over-looked Peter's feelings and let her own frustration take over. Children need us to acknowledge their feelings first—"Can you believe it? You were going to the bathroom, which is just what you were supposed to be doing, and your favorite blue shirt fell right in the toilet." This way Peter's mom would have gotten right into what was going on with Peter emotionally and participated in the event with him.

Then she could have helped *him* solve the problem. For example, Peter's mom could have said, "What if we write a note to remind us to wash that shirt when we get home, so it will be ready for you to wear tomorrow." The official look of a taped-up note would make Peter feel very important and confident that his shirt mattered.

Maybe Peter's mother didn't really understand why another shirt wouldn't do. We know that children between the ages of 2 and 4 often become bonded to things in some of the same ways they become attached to people. Peter's favorite blue shirt might feel so important to him that not being able to wear it when he wanted is a tremendous emotional loss. If we can understand that a young child's attachment to an item is very different from how we feel about it, it can help us approach such a situation with more patience and flexibility.

What about the teddy?

Maybe it's an inanimate object to us, but something like a teddy can be a very animate object to the child who communicates with it. Peter's whole day might be ruined without that good-bye kiss. We shouldn't just fluff over an emotional ritual and keep on moving, especially with a child of Peter's temperament. Just talking about it isn't enough. When we understand and respect the depth of children's emotions, we may be more inclined to think preventively. A solution might have been for Peter's parents to have one teddy that stays in the car and goes back and forth to preschool with Peter, and a different teddy that always stays home. An alternative might be to make the putting of Beboo in a special place a part of Peter's ritual when he wakes up or goes to bed. Many children love being responsible for putting a treasured object in a safe place, "right where it belongs," just the way they like having a safe place where they can belong.

Another strategy that might have eased Peter out the door would be for Peter's mom to have said, "Oh my gosh, we've run through the house and we can't find Beboo. But we don't have time to keep looking." She could pull out an envelope and say, "Put a kiss right in this envelope. I'm going to seal it and save it. When I get home after my appointment, I'm going to find Beboo and give him your kiss." To ease children's transitions, we need to take the time to reflect on their depth of feeling and do something with that insight.

What about a new approach?

For Peter's parents to take a few minutes that evening to reflect on the morning's chaos is not a luxury but a necessity. Otherwise, the same scenario could recur daily, with little variation.

Eliminating rushing is critical in easing young children's transitions. Maybe Peter's mom can set her alarm to go off 15 minutes earlier? Or his dad can get Peter dressed while his mom makes breakfast? By allowing extra time, problems that arise can be dealt with without the added stress of worrying about being late. Peter and his mother faced typical getting-ready-to-go problems. Next time maybe Beboo falls in the toilet, or Peter spills orange juice on his pants, or Peter's mom realizes the car needs gas. Whatever the cause, unless Peter's family has built extra time into their schedule, the morning is still disrupted.

Extra time also would have let Peter's mom explore how they each were feeling. They both were facing stressful events that day, plus the larger stress of Peter growing up and becoming more independent. Without time to explore these issues at the time, she could only wonder later: Was this particular program a good fit for him? *Did* Peter drop his shirt in the toilet on purpose? Were her feelings of relief at Peter's starting preschool normal? . . . There was a lot for her to think about.

Acknowledging the strong emotions of separation, and planning ahead as much as possible, can help create less stressful separation transitions. And that makes a young child's mastery of independence much easier for everyone.

3

Preparing for Separation

Above all, families need to feel comfortable about leaving their children. Aware, well-trained early childhood teachers can help both parents and children by devising separation procedures that fit everyone's needs and the particular environment. Details will vary from setting to setting. But an understanding of helpful practices benefits everyone. Everything teachers do must create a predictable, consistent environment for children and should inspire confidence in the parent when told with professional conviction, "Good-bye. Don't worry. We'll take good care of your child."

Anticipate, anticipate, anticipate

One teacher reminds us:

> "We have to prepare children for all kinds of things—like other crying children. My own first day of school, I remember a classmate crying hysterically; I wondered what he knew about this school that I didn't. The more children know about the first day of school, the better."

Both teachers and families need to anticipate what they likely will be encountering and ready themselves—for frazzled adults, upset children, and all the other typical stresses of a separation transition. With time, knowledge, and collaboration, teachers, children, and families can adjust to changing circumstances.

Arrange for family and teachers to talk

Parents and programs *both* must work to prepare children for a major change such as starting preschool—that is a given. But what parents can do is limited if the program is totally foreign to them.

Whether in the form of a workshop, social get-together, orientation tour, or family conference, a program needs to communicate with families about its policies and practices, preferably doing it in the company of other families. Parents may feel apprehensive, even panicky, at the prospect of leaving their child at preschool for the first time. They usually are reassured by talking to other parents and finding out they are not alone in feeling sad about saying good-bye. Digesting that message and dealing with those feelings is better done then, in the group, than at the classroom door the first day, when parents' tears are already beginning to spill over.

Whatever the format, teachers should explain the program and its policies, but should not do all the talking. Opening up discussion for everyone to share experiences lets teachers and parents get a sense of each other. This is the first step to a mutually trusting relationship and a lively classroom community. If teachers and parents share no common language, the program wants to find a way to meet parents' communication needs. For example, a sensitive bilingual college student—ideally from a nearby teacher education program—could help out.

One possible meeting structure would have teachers and parents sit together in a circle. Each person might describe a memory of confronting something unfamiliar—a new job, a first day at school, a party of strangers. (Participation is not mandatory; anyone may pass.) The discussion leader might ask, "What did you do to make yourself more comfortable? What did others do for you?" After discussing what makes adults comfortable, the conversation could move naturally to the group thinking of ways to adapt those ideas for young children.

Every early childhood program should have a separation policy (more on that in the next chapter), and distribute it on paper, as well as online, for families to take home and read at their leisure. (None of us can absorb highly loaded material in a single reading.) However, distributing a written policy is not a substitute for a well-designed, well-timed face-to-face meeting. Even after the meeting, teachers should touch base with families frequently, to reduce the chance of misunderstandings later.

The program should make sure families get any handouts or official documents in a language they can read, or that someone in their home community can read for them. Honoring a family's home language is always welcoming. As parents and their children approach a major separation event such as starting preschool, a special effort in this is crucial.

Ideally, any meeting should be sure to include *all* family members who will be responsible for dropping the child off at the program, as well as those who will be responsible for helping the child get ready in the morning. Programs can't assume only mothers will come. Invite everyone, especially fathers; and specifically think ahead about ways to make the men as well as the women comfortable. Think, too, about ways to make the visiting adults comfortable in the early childhood setting.

Sometimes, for example, it is disconcerting for adults to sit in child-sized chairs; it would be considerate to have standard chairs on hand.

A workshop, conference, or meeting has an important information function. But it has an interpersonal function, too. Rapport with teachers decreases parental anxiety, and vice versa. Establishing "reciprocal relationships" (NAEYC 2009) takes time, but families and teachers getting to know each other is where they start. If at this early occasion teachers demonstrate their willingness to learn from parents, and they begin to forge an alliance on children's behalf, the meeting will have achieved a most important purpose.

Have the teacher visit the family

Many programs have the teacher visit each entering child's home to begin establishing rapport with parents and child in an environment they find reassuring and familiar. During this early contact with the family, a teacher can begin finding out about the individual child—his or her idiosyncrasies, favorite foods, napping habits, beloved toys. Some teachers like to snap a photograph of themselves with the child to hang up in the classroom before the child arrives. Also, children can see for themselves that their parents and teacher are forming a relationship. This can support and encourage them in beginning to form their own relationship with their teacher. So begins an important *emotional triangle*. If it is a positive, trusting, respectful, consistent one, this three-way relationship of *parent-teacher-child* fosters in that young child feelings of security in classroom settings, for both present and future.

Some families find the idea of a teacher coming to their home intimidating or intrusive. Perhaps they worry their child will not behave "properly"— and he might not. A slow-to-warm-up child might choose to stay in her room. An attention-seeker might provoke a tussle with a sibling or refuse parental requests. But a teacher gains understanding from whatever happens. With experience, she can reassure the family, "It's okay" ... "I've seen it all before" ... "This behavior will most likely pass."

Other concerns could include exposing the family dynamic, or even the appearance of the home or neighborhood. Should a family feel really uncomfortable having the teacher visit, they can meet in a mutually convenient, neutral setting. It could be the preschool, but a local coffee shop, park, or library might be more appropriate. A place the child likes to go might be exactly the right choice for everyone.

Sound early childhood practice requires programs to pay their teachers to meet individually with families before the year begins. But for overworked teachers and cash-strapped programs, such a visit is not always possible. As a substitute, the teacher can write a letter to each family and include something special just for that child. One idea is a short welcoming note and photograph "so you'll recognize me on your first day." Then, even though the child has not met the new teacher in person, the letter and the photo are something tangible to excitedly show relatives and friends: "See, my teacher even wrote me a letter, and look how she signed her name, and she sent me a sticker on the envelope!"

Modern technology offers other options when a visit to the family isn't feasible. If families have access to the Internet, the program could create its own password-protected website. Then in a mailing to each family, the teacher could invite the child to visit the site to see her posted picture and message. From there the child could even send the teacher an email, which she could answer. Or the teacher can email the family directly with her message and photo.

Have the child visit the classroom

We might expect an anxious adult to stay calm entering a room full of strange people. But we certainly can't expect it of young children entering a new program, when they don't yet have the social and emotional skills to be intrepid. This makes an advance visit by the child to the classroom essential. No matter how inconvenient parents find scheduling a time for the child to visit, good practice requires it. Some programs go so far as making a visit mandatory—if a family can't conform to this basic requirement, then maybe the program isn't the right one for the family.

But it shouldn't come to that. Parents who are tuned in to the significance of a separation transition need to plan for it, just as they plan for other major emotional events in their family life. In an ideal world, their employers would plan for it, too, like they do when employees need time off for the flu or a funeral. Ideally, employers would *expect* parents to miss work while they ease their children into preschool (or other major change in setting), in recognition of the transition's importance as well as its stresses. Although a necessary developmental milestone, such a separation can be temporarily wrenching for family and child.

We—meaning our societal, collective "we"—need to educate not only parents but also employers to give priority to these crucial advance visits. Some employers, however, won't give an inch. That leaves the program to figure out new ways to meet families' needs, as in this example:

> "Our center serves low-income working families, mostly single parents, but we do insist on a school visit. Yes, it presents problems, but parents find a way to work it out. We schedule it at 7:00 a.m. or at 6:00 p.m. or on a Saturday, if necessary. We pay our staff for this extra time. The visit lasts one hour. No leaving [earlier]. Though this policy sounds inflexible, it supports children's best interests, and in the end helps the family, too."

What makes an advance visit so vitally important? From a visit, parents can absorb enough details to be able to answer children's later questions and to continue little by little their preparation between the visit and the first day. It's another occasion for parents and teacher to forge a partnership on behalf of the child and to address concerns before any issues develop. Parents can meet other families with children in the program, too.

For the children, having even a short preview of the physical space gives them images to think about at home. Children see where their teachers will greet them and where their parents will say good-bye, where the bathrooms are, and where they will eat their snack. They get a chance to meet their teacher and maybe even other children in the program. A mini-day of one or two open-ended activities when the child can briefly drop in and out would give families a small sense of what typically happens at the program and a chance to end the visit on a reassuring note at the pickup location. All things going well, it's a chance to get children excited about going off to preschool!

A visit can be just one parent and child alone, or as much as half the class as a group. But any visit should always include the opportunity for individual interaction between family and teacher. To extend the preview experience, teachers can lend or suggest books about going to preschool, and about separation issues generally, that parents can read at home with their children. (See the list of books for children in the Bibliography.) Parents and children might want to videotape themselves at school. Making the tape and watching it later at home is a chance for the family to talk about what's going to happen. Photographs taken during the visit are both a reminder for the child of this adventure and an opportunity to show everyone at home "my new school." Other ideas include children drawing what they saw on their visit and playing "Preschool."

4

The Adventure Begins

A child's first day exhilarates. It also provokes a myriad of conflicting feelings—pleasurable anticipation, uncertainty, tension—all wonderfully captured in Miriam Cohen's *Will I Have a Friend?* about an anxious boy's first day in kindergarten. Parents may feel ambivalent—happy to mark this childhood milestone, but nervous about how their child will fare in the world outside the family. Even if children have been in a child care setting as infants and toddlers, the preschool transition is typically a significant change. Children and families need guidance and support as they navigate this big, new adventure.

Who takes charge?

The program and its teachers should be responsible for setting the first day's tone and atmosphere and for establishing entry procedures and policies. Families and children are looking to them for clues to expected behavior—and should get those clues. It is more reassuring for everyone when teachers take the initiative, rather than leaving it up to children or allowing chance to dictate first interactions.

For example, after parents and child first arrive, the teacher's warm but authoritative invitation for parents to sit to the side in the classroom can signal what's expected: "For this first bit, please stay in one place so your child can find you. Let me draw your child out, so he can begin to make the attachment to me." If parents themselves jump in and begin playing with the blocks and the swings and the playdough, their child may conclude that this is a place where children and parents will play together.

Parents communicate that the classroom is a safe place to be when they are quiet observers, available to children as they face the unfamiliar, but not anxiously or protectively. Confidence is contagious. If teachers act confidently with parents, then parents will relax and display their confidence in the program to their children, who will feel more at ease in their new setting. While teachers need to take charge of the transition, they also must send parents the message that they are welcome in the classroom. Remember the relationship "emotional triangle"?

If more than one teacher is in the classroom, it may be helpful to assign each child and family to one teacher in particular. This way, each child and family can focus in the beginning on forming a relationship with just the one new adult. Conversely, the teacher will better get to know those children, and those parents will receive signals from the program from just one perspective.

How long should parents stay?

Once upon a time, many years ago, one of us brought her children to a highly regarded preschool where the other taught. The director had a saying for parents—"You love them, we'll teach them"—that explained the program's policy of not allowing parents beyond the threshold. Even now, as coauthors of this book, we're still upset by that policy, which so goes against what we know about children's separation stresses. For most 3- and 4-year-olds at that school, separation did not seem difficult, and some children immediately got over any initial anxiety. But other children paid a very high emotional price for such an abrupt transition. We wonder, how many graduates of that preschool (children *and parents*) still remember painfully that feeling when the parents had to leave their children at the door?

No program or teacher can predict which children will or will not be hurt emotionally by such a rigid policy, and so we recommend strongly against it. However, even if there was one best way for every child, sometimes real-world demands prevent a program from following it. And so, in this section, we acknowledge reality and suggest a compromising attitude to account for the variety of situations and personalities involved in deciding how long parents should stay: *It depends.*

Most in the early childhood field believe that a caring policy is one that allows parents to stay as long as necessary, especially if their child appears to need extra support. It should always be an available option for a parent to stay. We know that the reassuring presence of a child's attachment figure acts as a mediator between the safe and familiar and the scary and new.

But not everyone sees that principle as enough of a reason to allow parents to stay after dropping their child off. One family child care provider sums up her unequivocal position:

> "In my particular family child care program, it is better for parents not to stay because children adjust better without the parent there. I find a parent's presence too upsetting for the rest of the children in my small program, especially since children enter at different times."

Less sure is this director of a small rural program:

> "My teachers make [an advance] home visit to every single child. But then these 3-year-olds come on the bus alone for their first school experience. By and large, they do fine—much to my surprise."

Most teachers would try to dissuade parents from leaving immediately after drop-off. But whether it helps to let or encourage parents to stay over an extended separation period (e.g., "gradual enrollment") is a different question:

> "I worked in one school with a six-week gradual separation and much visiting—I don't know whether this prolonged period caused more anxiety or not. I'm not sure there wasn't more anxiety with the long separation process. Children [still] felt a loss of that parent in the classroom when the parent finally left."

No perfect policy exists for every child. Children are different; their temperaments vary. Not every child will experience separation with anger, sadness, or despair. Some children sail into a new setting without a backward glance. Younger siblings who might be slow to adapt in a different situation sometimes adjust easily because they heard what to expect from the sibling who entered earlier. Children who adapt easily may not understand why parents might stay but generally are fine with having them in the classroom.

Children who approach new experiences hesitantly may adapt better if parents remain longer. By staying they offer their child valuable support. But if they make themselves too available, the child may be reluctant to relate to classmates or teachers. "Be boring" is one good piece of advice for parents. If the parent appears less interesting to the child than all the exciting new people and things around him, the child may be more willing to

Take It Easy: Gradual Enrollment

Enrolling gradually means that a family member and the child together spend the first week getting to know [the teachers] and becoming familiar with the classroom for a little while each day. For the first few days the parent and child visit for a couple of hours, each day staying a little longer, with the parent perhaps leaving the room for some of the time when the child seems comfortable. By the end of the week the child should be ready to spend the day with a minimum of discomfort without the family member present.

This process entails a certain amount of inconvenience for working parents. Some use flex time to accommodate the gradual enrollment process. Others may turn to a close family member—a grandparent, for example—to help with the classroom visits or to care for the child later in the day. Encourage parents who are tight on time to spend at least the first two days visiting the classroom with the child.

Parents may be more eager to participate in gradual enrollment when they understand how important [a period of adjustment] is for their child's well-being. This initial getting-to-know-you period also helps acquaint parents with classroom routines and allows them to see the program's philosophy in action.

Excerpted from *Secure Relationships,* by A.S. Honig (Washington, DC: NAEYC, 2002), p. 52.

let go and join in on the activity. A parent who calmly reads a magazine on the sidelines lets that child know where she is, but doesn't give him the idea that they will be playing together in the classroom.

Some children are very attached to their home routines; they always want to go to the same playground, swing on the same swing, wear the same clothes. Such a child may be especially vulnerable to the idea that her parent who stayed that first day will always stay. Then when the parent finally leaves, she may feel more threatened than if the parent had never stayed at all. It's useful if families of children with such temperaments talk a lot with them about "how long until" and "what happens next." These children especially need to be clear about how long the parent will be staying. They need the truth: "Your teachers will let me sit quietly and read while you get used to things, but preschool is only for children. After I pick you up this afternoon, we can go to the playground and swing."

Circumstances vary as much as children's temperaments and family dynamics do. Children who haven't been in a group setting before or whose parents rarely left them may need a more gradual separation than children cared for within a large or extended family or who have been in child care with multiple caregivers.

Whatever the program's policy on staying is, good practice dictates that families be told in advance so parents, their children, and the teachers are prepared on entry day. Teachers should remind families to build some flexibility into their drop-off schedule for the first few days at least. Families should never arrive at the classroom door wondering what to do, or be unable to stay longer if the need arises.

What's the best way to leave?

"I've had parents say, 'She's playing so nicely, I'll just slip out.' How can children trust us if, in the first hour we're with them, we manage to lose the most important person in their lives?"

Whether it's after a few minutes, hours, or days, at some point the parent has to leave the child behind in the classroom. Not saying good-bye is sneaky. Even if it seems easier in the moment, it doesn't promote growth in the long run. Good-byes build trust. Saying good-bye each and every time strengthens children's belief that their parents will come back.

Parents, children, and teachers should have a general idea in advance of how the first good-bye will happen. Parents can ask their child beforehand, "How should we say good-bye? Do you want to give me a kiss or a hug?" It's reassuring for children to get a choice about the ritual, as they can't always control *when* the good-bye must come.

Once they arrive, many children soon branch out into the classroom environment, trying the sand table, taking a role in dramatic play, laughing with peers and teachers. Parents and teachers can even commend these children for their independence when they notice it. Ultimately, either teacher or parent will sense it is time for the parent to go. The parent might say, "I can tell that you're having a good time and that pretty soon you're going to say, 'Go home, and pick me up later.'" Cuing children to what's coming next can ease the separation process.

Parent and teacher should agree on a good time for the parent to leave, and make the child aware of it. A teacher could say, "Your mother will leave when the snack tray comes." Parents also can be the one to alert their child when they have to leave. If the child knows where the parent is going, so much the better. A simple strategy, as one teacher describes, may suffice:

> "I took my class up to see the room where some other parents were having coffee. More than a few of the new children said to their parents, 'Good-bye. Go have coffee with the moms and dads.'"

If circumstances absolutely prevent parents from staying for more than a few minutes, teachers must make an immediate connection with the child. It can help to swiftly focus the child's attention on an appealing activity. The parent might say, "I want to see your playdough sculpture when I pick you up. But now I need a good-bye hug because I have to go to work."

Eventually, we want the *child* to feel free to be the one leaving, rather than always the one being left. But that level of independence is an agenda for *life,* not the first day of preschool.

What kind of good-bye is best?

> Her mother was dropping off 3-year-old Sarah one morning at child care. After she kissed her daughter good-bye for the day, the little girl rubbed her lips vigorously with her hand. The mother moaned, "Sarah, why do you always wipe off my kisses?" To which her daughter replied, "Oh Mommy, I'm not wiping them off. I'm rubbing them *in."*

Good-byes matter. But almost any particular good-bye is fine, as long as it's part of a pleasant routine. Establishing a separation routine should begin before the first day, as part of the preparation that begins at home: "How should we say good-bye?" Programs can help a family establish a separation routine by making suggestions or helping them structure one that fits. In their orientation tour or workshop for new families, for example, teachers should explain how much comfort and security young children in stressful situations get from routines, and they can describe what supports the program will provide.

One idea is what many programs call a "cuddle couch" or a "cuddle chair"—a space by the exit where children and parents can say good-bye with words, hugs, and kisses. A wind-up music box, a sand clock, or a kitchen timer can help set limits once the routine is established. Like the teacher earlier with the snack tray, teacher or parent can say, "When the music stops … or the sand is finished … or the timer rings, it will be time to say good-bye."

Another structured routine might be for parent and child to pick something to read from a basket of *short* books near the exit; for example, Karma Wilson's *Mama Always Comes Home*. The two would enjoy the book together, then say good-bye in their own way. As the parent leaves to go out the door, the child leaves to put the book back where it belongs. Now it's time to play!

Teachers can invite children already in the program to be welcoming greeters of newcomers during their first few days. A peer can often engage a child more successfully than an adult, especially by suggesting specifically what the two might do together. For example, the teacher might ask Shaniqua to approach Benjamin, who is standing at the door, crying: "Why don't you ask him to help you feed Chi Chi the Rabbit?"

Even if a welcoming peer greeter also helps out, a teacher should always greet each new child individually. It helps ease children into the classroom setting when there is a greeting routine established at the door. The teacher should always welcome each child warmly and do something to acknowledge each personally. The greeting shouldn't be so repetitive that the child hardly notices and doesn't connect, but it should be predictable. For example, children could be asked each morning for their response or input:

> When Tommy and his mother arrived, they were greeted by Ms. Berman, clipboard in hand. "Oh Tommy, I'm glad you're here. We're having a survey: What's your most favorite thing to eat for breakfast?"

This experienced teacher knew to structure the question so she didn't have to hear each child's whole breakfast menu or didn't confuse or discomfort children who had eaten only one or two things (or even nothing!) when everyone else had eaten six. Later at Large Group she used the survey results to help the class begin to bond.

5

Separation Takes Time

As childhood milestones go, a young child's first day in the new setting is major. For parents, child, and teachers, all the weeks and months of preparation, all the feelings of anticipation and anxiety, peak. But a few days of adjustment—or longer, if enrollment is gradual, for example—isn't all there is to a successful separation transition.

Some children seem to slide right into preschool (or other major change in care setting). But maybe in three or four weeks—after they have tried all the new equipment, explored all the nooks and crannies, and checked out all the other children—they start missing their old life. They may miss the person they usually spend time with at home. Only after the novelty of the classroom has worn off does separation distress become an issue.

Other children move at a more cautious tempo. "Hesitant," "slow-to-warm-up," "shy," "young for her age"—these shouldn't be taken as persistent personality categories or permanent labels. But they may describe children who can thrive in a new setting given more time and extra support from families and teachers.

The point is that separation isn't a one-day event—or even a period that's over in a few weeks. It's an ongoing process of childhood. Anxiety will not vanish once and forever. With young children (and sometimes for their parents and teachers, too), upset feelings can be triggered or intensified by events. They might be typical on Mondays and Fridays, appear just before and just after vacations, maybe get worse during and after illnesses, when joint custody shifts, a favorite friend moves, a new baby is born, a teacher leaves. A child who cries on Wednesday may bound right in on Thursday, leaving his father to call after him, "Hey, wait for me!" We don't always know why.

All this may make early childhood programs sound like nothing but nonstop turmoil. They are not—although the emotionality of these occasions is not to be taken lightly. The message here for families and teachers is this: Observe carefully, respond sensitively, think flexibly, and avoid preconceived notions about the pace of a child's adjustment. The suggestions that follow apply anytime the need presents itself. With a thoughtfully planned and executed separation process, most children can live their group life together happily and productively without their parents in the room.

What can parents do?

What can parents do to help their child who's having a bout of separation distress? Normally young children find comfort in routines. But sometimes a change in routine, such as a different family member dropping the child off, can work wonders.

Parent and child planning a treat together may be an incentive to get through the separation. We're not suggesting a bribe ("Go to preschool today, and I'll give you a candy bar"). Instead, dad might say something like, "After I pick you up this afternoon, we'll go to the park." Or shop for school supplies or new shoes, or go for ice cream. Parents know what will work best for their child.

However, a promise of a treat, especially early pickup, should always be honored. Breaking such a promise can feel to children like a betrayal (even if the parent has a good excuse) or even like a trick to get them to stay longer.

What can parents say?

Separation issues can be very emotional. But because young children cannot yet fully articulate their anxieties or narrate their own emotional states, families should keep discussions about feelings simple. Children need the parent to listen carefully, accept what they say, and keep questions to a minimum. To an upset or worried child grandma can say simply, "It's hard to feel that way. I bet that pretty soon, you'll feel much better." Or, "I know you worry that I won't be here to pick you up, but I will be here." The goal is for children to be free of worries and not overly weighted down by talk about problems. A good approach is to offer examples of the child's past independence as a reminder: "Remember when you stayed at Pablo's house all afternoon? You had so much fun playing, and then I came for you just like I said I would."

Sometimes a child's crying or resistance is an expression of genuine fear or discomfort, and sometimes it is a strategy the child is using to get his way. If the behavior or emotional upset is simply manipulative, the adult can just insist, reasonably and firmly, "The plan is for you to stay."

When strong feelings are swirling around, as they often are during separation transitions, families help their child best to cope when they stay calm and consistent, offer encouraging words, and plan activities that support the child's developing independence.

How can programs bridge home and classroom?

A useful strategy for programs and teachers to ease children's transitions is to help families bring the familiarity of home to the classroom. The following policies and practices can do that:

Let the child bring items from home. As space allows, this might include blankets, stuffed animals, and favorite books. If the child has a space of her own—a cubby or a box for possessions—that will help.

Build on children's innate sensory awareness. Teachers can suggest the family put a scent from home onto a small piece of cloth. Then the cloth goes into a snack-sized resealable bag, not quite closed, so the child can open it easily. The scent might be a parent's favorite hand cream, perfume, or aftershave. In the morning, mom can tuck this bag into her child's pocket and say, "If you feel lonely today, take out your secret scent cloth. It will remind you that I'll pick you up later."

Make children feel like they matter. All children, but especially those having a hard time in a new setting, will find their place more easily when they feel they matter. Teachers can ask parents to collaborate in finding individual ways to give their child a special role or job in class with built-in, guaranteed success. For example, the child could hand out notices to each family as they arrive at school, or put the notices in every cubby for parents to take home. They might talk about how to spark a new interest, build on a current passion, or help the child become part of the existing group.

Engaging children in activities they enjoy encourages their enthusiasm for group life. As the classroom becomes a community, teachers can extend the ideas with suggestions from the children themselves. For example, before the year begins, maybe during the home visit, child and teacher can figure out an activity that might engage the child from the first day in his new setting. It is especially helpful if parents and teachers can share the responsibility for having materials ready when the child arrives. Or the child might suggest a favorite activity that she loves to do at home, and bring it to school.

Reassure children using their developing sense of time. With young children, teachers can use non-clock time to mark intervals: "Your father will be back after Outside Time." They could talk about what will happen next, but also about where the parent is now and what he may be doing in relation to the child's developing day. This keeps the bridge between home and classroom lively.

Encourage children to engage in dramatic play, at home and in the classroom. Teachers can act out future or past events with children using dolls and role play, and help families to do the same at home. Such play can decrease children's anxiety as they work through what is happening to them in real life through their fantasy. Imaginary conversations on prop telephones in the dramatic play area can help children to talk about their feelings. Keyboards might prompt a distressed child to "type mommy a letter about leaving me here." At home, it might generate a typed complaint about "Casey at school, who pushed me at Snack." Both would be opportunities for teachers and parents to follow up with the child, with each other, or both, in a later discussion.

Use modern technology. First, a caveat: So many new possibilities exist to connect home and the classroom that all the adults in a child's life could spend the entire day in touch electronically. Technology can easily become intrusive, so a program must consider carefully which devices and policies contribute best to children's healthy development. Factors to be considered include technical expertise, cost, and privacy.

Here are some increasingly sophisticated possibilities:

Telephone—Allow a child to call, if the parents have said it's okay. Children can get a lot of comfort from an occasional chat with a sorely missed parent. For some children, leaving a message may be comfort enough.

Photographs—Familiar images can bring children comfort. They can wear a parent's picture on their clothing (e.g., as a pin or patch), or hang up pictures of their pet or house somewhere in the classroom. A wall of family photos can be a nice project for the whole group.

Audio/video recordings, CDs/DVDs—Video or audio recordings of home and family can be kept in an accessible place in the classroom and played as needed. When child and teacher share no common language, a CD, video, or audiotape in the child's home language can be especially important in adding a comforting familiarity to the day. Parents can record directions for naptime and other routines in the family's home language for teachers to play, so the child will know what to do.

Email—Allow children to email. The act of writing the message or dictating one to a teacher and then hitting Send can soothe a child.

Instant media—Some programs, families, and teachers may be savvy enough to send images to a teacher's phone from their own and vice versa. Another technology is webcams, where children can view their parent at work or home, or the adult can view the child in the classroom.

6

Going Home: Another Separation

So far we have mostly described a young child's separation transition *from* home and family attachment *to* preschool. But there is another transition to consider—the daily transition children must make from the classroom *back home.*

At the beginning of each day, their teachers invite children to join them in a stimulating environment and a new community of adults and peers. In a quality program, novel activities and other experiences develop each child physically, cognitively, and creatively, while being fun, too. If the child's teachers are nurturing and consistent and sensitive to his needs, they also can become additional attachment figures in his life. It's a setting that requires big steps in a child's growth. Transitioning home is part of the emotional growth process. Teachers play an important role in helping children end that daily experience and rejoin their families successfully.

Two factors at the end of the day complicate this process: Children often are physically and emotionally exhausted after all their new experiences, and emotions can run high as parents and children realize how much each may have missed the other.

Young children need to repeatedly experience reunions that are calm and caring and that leave them feeling comfortable, secure, and confident. Such reunions build a healthy foundation for children's future independence. It is through the cycle of exploring and returning to home base, where they gain confidence, that children gradually move out into the world.

Managing and expressing feelings

After hours apart, nothing warms a parental heart more than to be greeted by a happy child who rushes to give hugs and kisses and cheerfully prepares to go home. It happens that way, but not always. Some daily reunions are much less satisfying. What are parents to think when their child procrastinates about leaving with them? When he acts as if seeing the parent appear in the doorway doesn't matter much? When she won't let go of her teacher's hand and take the parent's outstretched one? When angry or sad feelings about being left that morning or missing mommy—in check the whole day away from home—overflow and the child cries or acts out?

When reunions go badly in this way, sometimes a parent's first impulse is to respond with frustration, anger or hurt, even rejection or detachment. But the adults in the child's life need to put themselves in her position, to try and understand what she may be feeling. It is important they have some understanding of how attachment works, as well as what children's social/emotional development is like around preschool age.

Without those understandings, such behavior by their child at pickup time may lead parents to feel that their child prefers the classroom over home. Even worse, they may resent the attachment they see between teacher and child or even fear the teacher's bond is displacing theirs.

It doesn't help that at the end of a long day everyone is tired. None of us is at our best when we're tired or stressed. And we all—children and adults alike—sometimes can feel anxiety and loss when cut off from home

---

Understanding Teacher-Child Attachments

If they aren't familiar with attachment theory, families sometimes need help understanding the value of letting their child bond with her teachers. (It is particularly valuable for very young children and their caregivers.) Strategies such as the following are a good place for the program and teachers to start:

Talk about attachment at the initial interview or as soon as a family enters the program.

Help parents understand children's need to form attachments with the special adults in their lives. Explain that a young child is able to bond with *multiple* significant adults.

Celebrate the primary attachment between parents and their child. Caution parents against behaviors that destabilize that connection, such as sneaking out without saying good-bye.

Talk about children's happiness, how they thrive when they are with adults they care about and who care about them. Connect this to brain development and identity formation. Show how attachment frees children to focus more on developmentally appropriate tasks of childhood and builds the foundation they need for higher-level thinking as they approach age 5.

Explain that high-quality teachers are distinguished by their ability to bond with other people's children. But also share what professional lines the program draws to keep teacher-child attachments respectful of family bonds, appropriate, and constructive.

Adapted from *Relationships, the Heart of Quality Care,* by A.C. Baker and L.A. Manfredi/Petitt (Washington, DC: NAEYC, 2004), pp. 57–8.

or when in a strange environment. Add to that children's stress of having little control over their situation.

Children need parents to acknowledge these deep feelings, and if they neglect to, children will remind them:

> "When my child was at nursery school, he would have an instant tantrum when I arrived to pick him up. Of course, as a parent I was mortified. One day he walked away from me and down the street—peeling his clothes off along the way until he was stark naked. Yes, he came back. And I gave him a big hug. But he certainly made his anger dramatically clear, maybe in the only way he could."

All of us want children to grow up feeling secure. Part of that emotional security is for children to expect to get support from their attachment figures when they are out of sorts or anxious, or when life circumstances intrude on their emotional safety. It takes a village of collaborators to achieve this at the end of the day. Parents know their own children best; teachers bring experience over many parent-child reunions. Everyone benefits when the adults share information and help interpret children's behavior for each other. For example, parents may notice that at home their child shows joy at seeing them when they arrive, and may recognize that the absence of that joy at pickup time could be a clue to something amiss. Other parents know their child is reserved and matter-of-fact in both contexts and so don't worry. But teachers need to know all that to understand children's behavior and emotions.

Supporting children as they work through negative feelings is an important part of early childhood leadership. Sometimes parents may not be aware that their child is angry or sad or may not know where the upset might be coming from. Teachers can help parents and children identify strong feelings and work through them together. Here's a good example of teacher and child collaborating to make a reunion more successful:

> Leila was stomping around furiously at the end of the day, but I was intentionally gentle when I asked, "Are you upset because your father is late?" Asking rather than asserting is a more respectful approach.
>
> "Yes, I'm angry. Jasmine left already," Leila replied and began to cry. I expanded on what she said: "And you don't want to be here for a long time after your best friend has gone?" Leila nodded.
>
> Clearly she recognized that I had understood. Leila came closer and held my hand while she dried her eyes with a tissue. As she relaxed, I proposed that she and I have a *conference* with her father when he arrived, to tell him what just happened. When her father arrived, Leila ran to him, practically shouting, "Let's have a *kong-fence,* and I'll tell you about how I just pounded my feet all over the floor. I don't like it here by myself!"
>
> After this outburst, Leila's father agreed to sit right down, and we helped him to understand his daughter's vivid message. For the most part, he picked Leila up on time the rest of the year. I didn't have to tell this parent directly that his lateness was upsetting to Leila. Instead, I provided a constructive way for Leila to express her own feelings, a way for her to take care of herself emotionally. Adults can underestimate young children's capabilities for positive resolutions.

This teacher's solution helped both child and family address his sadness:

> The first two days of preschool, Hector was the last child to be picked up. Both days his mother rushed in late, apologized matter-of-factly, and greeted him with a sheepish smile, which Hector didn't return. The third day, Hector started crying the minute I announced Clean-up Time. Hector had been fine all day, and I realized he might be anticipating a repeat of the last two pickups. "Are you crying because you think your mother might be the last to come?" Hector emphatically nodded yes through soft, gulping sobs.

By this time, most of the other children had left. I sat down near Hector and reached into my apron pocket for the self-adhesive nametags I always carry. I suggested we write some messages that he could wear. I suggested that the first one could say, "I've been crying, I'm sad." He smiled at that idea, so I wrote that out, and he immediately stuck the nametag on the front of his shirt, then gestured to the remaining ones.

"Do you think the next one should say why you've been crying?" Hector grabbed my pen and scribbled all over a second nametag, stuck this one also on his shirt, and reached for another. I didn't disrupt the flow of his energy to ask what these nametags said; his tears had subsided and Hector clearly knew what he was expressing.

When his mother arrived, Hector dashed to her and showed her all of the messages he was proudly wearing. This little boy had needed an outlet for his overwhelming emotions. I told his mother why we had been writing the notes. She got the point and made every effort to be on time from then on. Sometimes she even came a little early, and Hector rewarded her with a smile and a great big hug.

Another child might require a different response to end-of-the-day emotions:

Referring to the traffic that was making her mother late for pickup, Melissa looked out the window and said tearfully, "I love my mommy, but I hate my mommy's car!"

Love and loyalty prevented Melissa from thinking or saying she was angry at her mother directly; she was more comfortable blaming the inanimate car, the "mommy-delivery vehicle." Releasing negative feelings is healthy, as is expressing needs clearly. To adopt the child's vantage point and focus on the car, rather than on the parent, would be a safe response. With that in mind, Melissa's teacher might ask, "Would you like my help in talking to your mom about that car? Maybe we can make it come on time."

Reestablishing special bonds

Like a drop-off routine, the end-of-the-day reunion creates an occasion for bonding, sets the stage for easier transitions later on, and gives parents and teachers an opportunity to interact.

Parents and child need to work out a routine that lets both reestablish the unique bonds between them. Children all reconnect differently, and they need the parent to be available in a way that works best for them. For some children, reconnecting needs to be gradual, and a good place to begin is probably a gentle, nonverbal overture: comforting hand on the child's shoulder, rub on the back, request for a hug. Some children are more comfortable when the parent pays attention to what's going on in the classroom; for example, "I see you're painting with blue paint today." Other children more easily reconnect over a discussion about "what's next," such as stopping at the store on the way home. It's an important parental job to figure out what suits a child most.

It may be best for teachers to stay out of the way of an effusive child running toward her mother. But an experienced teacher can certainly make the going home transition easier for a child who hangs back. For the child who can't seem to get going, the teacher might suggest a physical image or action to encourage him to move toward the door: "We learned about kangaroos today. I think I see one in the backseat of your mom's car" or "Do you think you can hop like a kangaroo all the way to the parking lot?"

A teacher might drop a detail about the day to bridge the classroom-home transition and open a topic for child-parent conversation: "Be sure to tell mom what you did to take care of Juanita's scraped knee," or "On the way to the car, why don't you tell grandma what we found growing in our vegetable garden today?" Another idea is to invite the parent to join in the child's world: "I think your dad might want to see the grocery store you helped build in the block corner. Do you want to show him?"

Usually just a detail is enough. Parents need to know something about the day, so they can start a conversation. But a considerate teacher honors the parent-child bond by letting a child's family hear about his big accomplishments from him. One stress on families of young children in school or child care is feeling like they always miss the childhood milestones. Hearing from their child about the first time Jack "writes" his name, and Hun catches the ball, and Majeeda ties her shoes is more meaningful than a teacher announcing to an arriving family, "Guess what I saw your child do today?"

If the child ignores that the parents have arrived, or seems distant, the teacher can reassure them that their child really did miss them. A knowledgeable teacher might point out that some very young children have a hard time switching focus. To break through a child's muted greeting, parents could make immediate physical contact: "I missed you, so I need an extra hug *right now*, okay?" Or ask a direct question about what the child is doing or about a detail the child cares about: "How did you get that shade of blue on your painting? Was it hard?" or "What did you have for snack today?"

Sometimes it's the child who's disappointed by the parent's demeanor, and it's the adult who needs the teacher's help to reconnect and reenergize. A family child care provider tells this story:

> "I had a parent who arrived every day with a scowl on her face. One day I said, 'Try coming in with your great smile, and let's see how your little one reacts. Your smile could melt away anyone's worn-out mood.' You know, she hasn't missed a day of smiling since."

This is a reason why pickup is not the time for a teacher to recount a child's impossible behavior earlier in the day. Instead of getting the nurturing reunion the child needs, he gets a disappointed, irritated parent. Nor is this the time for parents to raise concerns about the schedule or the quality of the program. Parents should raise such issues later in a phone call, email, or family conference.

Remember, successful reunions build the foundation for children's future independence—but to be successful, those reunions need to feel calm and safe.

7

Uneasy Separations

Attachment theory tells us that young children's protests at being separated from their attachment figure usually are a healthy response, a sign of a strong emotional bond. Even when children's reactions are upsetting (and what crying isn't), it helps families and teachers to know that such behavior is usually brief and that most children will be calm and engaged within a reasonable amount of time. That understanding gives perspective when the program, family, and teacher have done everything "right"—home visits, program visits, gradual enrollment, comforting pickup and drop-off routines—yet the child's separation transition still is unsuccessful.

Troubled separations can take different forms, depending on family dynamics, a child's temperament, the classroom tone, and so forth. Upset behaviors are not necessarily a problem if they occur rarely or briefly, and they are mild, and the child can be comforted. It's when they persist, or are intense or disturbing, or the child is inconsolable that family and teachers must reexamine the situation.

Difficulty settling in

For parents, turning away from an upset child may rank among life's most unpleasant experiences. No matter how prepared a parent may be, it's emotionally hard to pry loose from a crying child, especially one who's yelling, "Don't leave me! I want to go home!" The goal in early childhood settings is to avoid this trauma if we can. But sometimes a child seems settled, only to begin crying after the parent leaves. Sometimes the distress starts at drop-off and just doesn't stop, or only gets worse once the parent is gone.

Teachers need to acknowledge the child's feelings and offer comfort— even if that comfort is hard for the child to accept at the time. But variation in individual circumstances makes it difficult to generalize about what else to do without more information: Does the child have a history of controlling adults with tears? Are the child's tears steady or intermittent? Has there been gradual enrollment? Is the child getting sick? How far away is a parent? Parents and teachers need to collaborate on solutions that not only support the child's growth but also work for the family and the program.

Programs should have a policy—or, better yet, a mutually convenient arrangement with each family—about how and when to communicate about an inconsolable child. Family and program should agree beforehand whether the parent will call or email the teacher to check in during the day, or whether the teacher will report within a specified timeframe if the child stays upset. Parents who leave a very distressed child may want to call the teacher, if only to relieve their own anxiety. Most teachers tend to agree with this mother:

> "You know me, I would want to go back after 30 minutes of his hard crying. Why should the other children at school suffer? And, more important, why should my child suffer?"

A child who is inconsolable might need a temporary accommodation such as an early pickup, especially in the initial days of a new program, when a new baby is born, or some other family disruption is adding stress. If the child continues to be highly distressed when the parent leaves, the parent may need to stay at school longer than is typical, until that particular child is ready to separate. If that is impossible, perhaps an extended family member or family friend can sit in the classroom until the child is ready to join the rest of the group without a familiar adult nearby.

Anxious attachments

Children get a lot from a loving child-parent bond, including feelings of comfort and security, self-confidence, and help with self-regulation (Honig 2002). Families and teachers who understand these benefits of attachment hope for a similar bond to form between child and teacher. And it does for many children who make successful separation transitions.

But when that parental bond isn't the best, or the child or parent is ambivalent about separation, for example, then a healthy child-teacher bond has trouble forming. Whatever the reason, teachers need strategies in their repertoire to help solidify their relationship with each child.

Some children resist attaching themselves to new adults. Teachers should respect children's need for initial distance. But sometimes a child covers anxiety by avoiding the teacher. If, in a reasonable time, the child refuses to interact, it is important they find a way to get closer to each other. For example, the teacher might pique a special interest, make the child her assistant for half an hour one morning, or devise a situation that requires the two to become partners. Careful observation is key, as this example demonstrates:

Jose's teacher used happenstance to melt his serious resistance to her. One day, walking together down the long, tiled corridor that led to the playground, she taught him how to call out "Woo-woo" then listen for the sound of his own voice in the echo. After that, Jose willingly became her hand-holding partner for those two minutes in the corridor each day. His delight in the sounds was the beginning of a relationship that in time eradicated his avoidance.

Other children do the opposite and refuse to leave the teacher's side. Bowlby and other researchers have taught us that rebuffing a child's attachment behavior is likely to his heighten anxiety and anger. Ignoring children's distress does not promote self-reliance. One teacher describes that dilemma and how she solved it:

"I had a parent who brought her son, Jason, to school only occasionally. When she wanted his company, she kept him home. To no one's surprise, Jason adjusted badly to school. When he came, he attached himself exclusively to me and there he stayed.

"The first two weeks, Jason stuck to me like glue. At first I tried to discourage his attachment, but when that didn't help I changed my approach. I told him, 'When I leave the room or wash my hands or go outside, you can come if you want, or don't.' My ultimate goal was to move him out into the classroom, but what I was really saying to him was, 'I believe you have the strength to adapt, and when you are ready to join in activities without my physical presence, you will.' Little by little, he began to separate. He played with other children for longer and longer periods. By June, Jason was ready to leave me entirely, happy to go on to the next class."

Here's another suggestion for dealing with a child who is "shadowing"—by giving her a feeling of importance and an incentive to move into the group:

s home, sit down and have a private chat.
g to believe what will happen tomorrow
be all ears. "There's going to be a special
ect. Until you get to school tomorrow, that
use you're going to be in charge of that table,
can remove the cloth."
ren who arrive early will want to know what's
n't know until Crystal arrives. The minute
ou ready for your special table?" Crystal's
anticipation of Crystal lends an element of

he dynamics in the room. This ploy lets her
ces her the center of attention by starting the
t with other children. Children need to branch
this strategy connects her to a table, to a sur-
—all of which permit her to grow away from
adowing.

t home and in the classroom in order to feel
ld. An anxious child, for example, is more
her attachment figures than a fearless, con-
ith knowledge of child development, will
nd teacher about when a child is ready to be
dence, or needs to be held closer.
not incompatible with sound, nurturing early
childhood practice to recognize that children sometimes use tears and other
symptoms of distress to try to control adults. To not be drawn into these
manipulative games, teachers have to plan ahead and devise strategies
that instead promote children's growth. We do more for children when we

continuously ask ourselves what will create more self-reliance within each child, than when we just let them shadow us.

Delayed responses

Whether the cause of distress is a new baby or not, children sometimes worry about what is going on with their family in their absence.

> "My mommy's home with my new baby brother, and maybe they're having fun without me."

Maybe after a few weeks, once the novelty of the new playground, new friends, and new toys wears off, the child realizes how much he misses home. Maybe, all of a sudden, he realizes that he'd rather have his father—not these new teachers—bandage his scraped knee. He would rather play at home with a friend, with his own toys. He's tired of having to share and bend to program norms.

Such realizations are a classic cause of new tears, even in a child who entered the program without any hesitation and adjusted successfully. Just as they did at the beginning of the year, children need reassurance when this kind of thing happens. And, just as if it were the beginning, children may need their parents to spend some time with them transitioning all over again.

As we do for other manifestations of unsuccessful or difficult separation, we always encourage children to express their feelings. Depending on the child, the teacher and parents might encourage her to dictate a note to take home about how she's feeling, act out her feelings about the situation with hand puppets, read stories about feelings (see the Bibliography for suggestions), talk to other children, and the like.

Looking for causes of extra stress

It's human nature to fear abandonment. It's what gives power to the threat we all have heard frustrated parents use.

> "If you don't come right now, I'm leaving without you."

But young children cannot yet differentiate between an empty threat and its reality. The panic on a child's face, the quick move to follow, reveal it all. Even if their parents never do leave them, the thought that they might can create enormous anxiety. Even seemingly confident children can be left frightened at some deep level.

Children facing a separation already wonder, "Can my parents be counted on? Will they really come back, or might they be really gone this time?" If their parents are users of the "I'm leaving" threat, children's stress may be even greater. But when a child is distressed at separation, and the adults can't figure out why, a teacher can hardly ask, "Do you threaten your child with abandonment?" Nor do parents rush to confess how frequently they may do exactly that.

Teachers can, however, help families to understand young children don't know that their parents won't really abandon them. They also can suggest better ways to deal with dawdling children. For example, to encourage a child to hurry up, mom could say, "Do you think we can get your shoes on and be in the car before we count to 30? Let's try. One, two…!" Better to make the time it takes getting out the door fun, rather than filled with tension and tears.

An insensitive message that's nonverbal also can add to a child's separation stress. What if a parent arrives in the morning to see all the other children playing happily, while her child is clinging to her for dear life. Maybe her impulse is to push him away from her and toward the group. She may even think it's encouraging. But she might as well have said out loud, "Why are you the only one who can't separate?"

We never want to communicate to young children that they are not okay, that they don't measure up. Parents must exercise considerable self-control to avoid indulging such impulses. Teachers can help by talking about the situation, offering alternative strategies, and reassuring the family to keep faith that their child will probably adjust eventually. Not sending young children negative messages about themselves not only improves the separation process but also is important in supporting their healthy emotional development.

Thinking together

What if a child hasn't been able to ease into the group setting after a few weeks, or seems to have transitioned successfully only to fall apart later? When the usual adjustment techniques aren't helping, then family and teachers need to explore the possible reasons.

Teachers may appropriately ask families for information about a child's home life as they search together to explain current behavior. However, no family should feel compelled to share beyond their comfort level. While communication is imperative, a joint family-teacher effort to solve a problem is not an invitation for the teacher to play therapist or to make families feel invaded. The balance is delicate between family privacy and a teacher's need to have a full picture of the child. But with the child's welfare at stake, trying to find that balance is vital.

Teachers might begin by asking a family member, "You know your child better than we possibly could. Can you guess what might be going on in Dominic's life to cause these behaviors/feelings?" Parents may have instant insight. If not, a few relevant questions can further the conversation. For example, "At home, have your brief separations or evenings out been difficult?" "Have you had to take any overnight business trips?" "Has Dominic had to change where he lives due to a move or custody arrangement?" "Is there a new baby?" "Has a pet or any person close to him or to others in the family died?" "Can you think of any other stressful circumstances in his life lately?"

Young children thrive on familiar routine, predictability, and continuity of care. Sudden changes such as shifting family dynamics, new environments, numerous caregivers, and the loss of a family member are stresses that cause emotional reactions. We can expect separation to take more time. Empathetic teachers can help minimize the pain of such experiences by showing warmth, comfort, and understanding—not just to the child but to all members of the family.

Providing that support can sometimes be a challenge. All early childhood teachers at some point will encounter complex family circumstances that make it almost impossible to support the child adequately. This example suggests how hard it can be for teachers to accept their limited ability to improve a child's upsetting home life:

> "We had a wonderful child at our school. We don't have him anymore because mom took him out. When she got married, the new husband didn't want a child around, so the father took him. Then mom took him back and unloaded him on grandma, who didn't want him either. Grandma was angry at mom to the point where she just dumped this kid on our steps and shoved him in the door. We turned around, and there he was. Talk about separation—it took real effort to get him out of his aggressive state and receptive to us."

Teachers are ethically and legally obligated to report circumstances where they suspect there may be abuse or neglect. But in a family melodrama like this, what support can teachers provide? What's important is to stay neutral in the conflict. Children shouldn't have to worry about whose side their teachers will take, or the consequences of adult biases, or what teachers might repeat to others. We can't make life right for all children, but the classroom can be a safe harbor for them to come to every day. A stressed child needs his teachers to listen calmly to whatever he wants to tell them without judging. They help a child when they encourage her to express her feelings freely, in oral stories or with drawings, puppets, or dolls, for example.

Another possible reason for continued separation distress is that the family is pushing the child "out of the nest" too soon.

> Suppose you do all these things and none work. A child is still upset, crying, without joy or pleasure in your classroom. This may signal that perhaps he or she needs the added boost of a parent's presence in the classroom again. [But] where a parent's return makes the situation worse, it may be that the child is not ready for a group experience at all. In such a case it might be better to suggest delaying the entry for a short time. (Balaban 2006, 63)

After all, children develop differently; some children are ready to separate at an earlier age than others are. When a child doesn't transition successfully to preschool, teachers need to help parent and child (and sometimes themselves) recognize that no one has "failed."

> There is no such thing as failure in early education entry. There may be only a slipping back, which requires help. (63)

Seeking outside advice

Most children resolve their separations successfully. But some don't, and it's not clear why. The stress of not knowing what next steps to take only makes an already upsetting situation worse. Sometimes just sharing problems in a parenting discussion group or with a good listener can bring a family new insight. Sometimes advice from a specialist may be in order.

Professional help might be necessary if, after several weeks, a young child consistently refuses to separate; exhibits nervous habits, meltdowns, extreme moodiness, or uncharacteristic behavior; or is withdrawn or depressed. In fact, as worrisome as an inconsolable child who is howling in the center of the room may be, in the long run the despairing, detached, silently suffering child is much harder to help.

If parents don't reach out on their own when the need for a professional seems clear, it may be appropriate to intervene. A teacher or program administrator should choose a quiet, calm moment to broach the topic, using utmost tact, gentleness, and restraint. A beginning might be: "Sometimes it's so hard to be objective about our own children that I thought I'd ask whether you would like to talk to someone about Julie's resistance to preschool?" Or "Would you consider asking a therapist if she could help Hector be happier at school?" Sometimes a self-disclosing admission is a good approach: "When my child was little and refused to separate from me, I asked a professional to help. Those suggestions got us past our difficulties."

When a family is receptive to the idea, the program (or pediatrician or clergy member) can recommend a parenting coach, child therapist, social worker, psychologist, psychiatrist, or other professional suited to the situation.

8

Partnering in Children's Separation

To make a successful separation transition to preschool (or other child care setting), a young child needs to be part of the trusting, respectful three-way relationship that we earlier called the *emotional triangle*. For that parent-teacher-child relationship to form and flourish, the adults must act in partnership on the child's behalf. The partnership is so important for young children that "establishing reciprocal relationships with families" is one of the five guidelines that inform developmentally appropriate practice for early childhood educators (NAEYC 2009, 16).

A "reciprocal relationship" means parents have a significant role to play, as this teacher explains:

> "If we take on the role of 'superteachers' who know it all, we discount the abilities of parents and avoid the possibilities of genuine partnerships. When we talk about 'educating families,' we can't be the *we* who educates *them*. Instead, we must say to parents, 'I rely on you—you are the most important person in your child's life.'"

How to Foster Reciprocal Relationships with Families

1. Reciprocal relationships between practitioners and families require mutual respect, cooperation, shared responsibility, and negotiation of conflicts toward achievement of shared goals.

2. Practitioners work in collaborative partnerships with families, establishing and maintaining regular, frequent, two-way communication with children's parents.

3. Family members are welcome in the program and participate in decisions about their children's care and education.

4. Teachers acknowledge a family's choices and goals for children and respond with sensitivity and respect to those preferences and concerns, without abdicating professional responsibility to children.

5. Teachers and the family share their knowledge of the child and understanding of children's development and learning as part of day-to-day communication and planned conferences. Teachers support families in ways that maximally promote family decision-making capabilities and competence.

Adapted from "Developmentally appropriate practice in early childhood programs serving children from birth through age 8" (NAEYC Position Statement, adopted 2009) in *Developmentally appropriate practice in early childhood programs serving children from birth through age 8*, 3d ed., eds. C. Copple & S. Bredekamp, 1–31 (Washington, DC: NAEYC), p. 23.

But it also means that teachers don't abdicate their professional responsibility by doing whatever a parent wants regardless of whether or not they agree that it is in the child's best interest.

To truly partner with them, teachers should see family members as individuals, value their experiences, and enter into a trusting, friendly alliance with them on behalf of the child. The same is true in reverse, for parents. As teachers and parents get to know each other through informal daily contact, meetings, and parent conferences, their relationship grows stronger.

Acknowledging parents' mixed feelings

Life for families today is a balancing act between home, work, and school that takes an emotional as well as a physical toll. The mother of a 2-year-old feels that pressure:

> "I can best liken my life—as a daughter, mother, child care teacher, administrator, and student of child development—to being in the middle of a four-way cloverleaf freeway exchange, monitoring traffic as it goes in all different directions at once."

Most of America's preschoolers, in single- and two-parent families alike, have parents who work outside the home, meaning that the child is in some form of care or school setting at least part time. Family circumstances don't always let children start a new program at a developmentally optimal time for them. Parents putting their child into a program can be left feeling a mix of emotions, including guilt, relief, sadness, regret, even jealousy.

> "I understand all the socioeconomic and societal changes that have brought me to this place. But that doesn't transform the discomfort I feel when I leave my 2-year-old daughter in child care, even (and especially) when she cheerfully waves 'Bye-bye' to me."

From the beginning, an early childhood teacher needs to recognize that to hand over their child, even for part of the day, can be a source of parental anxiety. A question from a parent such as "How come Adam is so good with you and not with me?" may be a clue that the parent feels some rivalry or jealousy. An empathetic response might be, "I don't take care of your child *better* than you do. Our roles are different."

A parent's offhand comment, such as "I don't know where you get the patience to put up with Zenia's unruliness day after day," may imply envy of the caregiver's competence. The teacher might tell this parent: "My education prepared me to deal with all kinds of behavior. Do you want to brainstorm some strategies?" Questions such as "Why does he come home so dirty?" or "Why can't you make her nap?" may be reflections of parental anxiety, too. That a teacher often spends more waking hours with their child than the parents do only magnifies such feelings.

Experienced, empathetic teachers see behind such complaints and questions to the parent's wish for a more intimate role in the child's classroom life. Rather than regarding the comments as intrusive or critical, they can hear them as an expression of a parent's desire to participate in decisions affecting the child's welfare. That interest should be met with straightforward answers and explanations. Just like their children, parents are having to adjust to a new situation, and that stress sometimes comes out as anxiety, which typically fades as the surroundings become more familiar—and as new, positive relationships develop.

Even though parents may understand intellectually that teachers are not in competition with them for their child's affections, emotionally it can be difficult to keep insecurities at bay. Teachers can make a habit of reassuring them: "You are the most important person in your child's life." It's something that parents can't hear enough. However, we want children and their teachers to develop bonds. Sometimes parents forget or don't understand that a positive attachment benefits everyone, and teachers should remind them. But teachers also should acknowledge frequently that the connection to a parent is a child's most basic, and that connection can never be replaced.

Respecting each other to prevent and solve problems

Anytime their child first enters preschool, a family may feel uncertain about how that child will be received, especially if they or their child is "different" from the other families or children. Difference can take many forms, including physical, cultural, circumstantial (e.g., socioeconomic status, family configuration, parents' sexual orientation), and behavioral (e.g., child's maturity, capacity to conform to expectations). Coping with feeling different can be an added source of pressure, both during the process of separation and beyond. But whatever those differences may be, teachers and families share a responsibility to work through the pressures together.

Teachers and parents do not have to become best friends. But if they work to develop mutual trust, everyone becomes more open about discussing problems. They can speak more freely, because each will better understand what was *meant* (rather than what may have been *said*) and so are less worried about offending each other. Then, when problems arise, they are easier to work out. And problems *do* arise:

> Carmen was absent 46 days during her first year. Her parents did not feel the slightest bit negative about separation, and Carmen adjusted well. But her family would keep her home to visit her grandparents, as company when her brother was sick, and for any number of family occasions. The teachers complained that "her parents didn't seem to care about Carmen's education." Her parents felt put down by the teachers. When Carmen did come, the adults rarely talked.
>
> As the next year began, the absences continued. But Carmen's new teacher perceived her family differently. At pickup and drop-off times, the

teacher saw a strong, tightly knit Hispanic family, fiercely protective of their cultural values. The teacher made an effort to let the family see that he knew Carmen well and how much Carmen loved school. So when he approached her parents to discuss the excessive absences, the conversation went well.

"I know we all want what's best for Carmen," he said. And they could trust he meant it. "But now that she's older, there's so much more she needs to be learning." He made some suggestions for activities the family might do with Carmen when they did keep her at home, and they agreed to keep her home much less often.

Notice that the teacher did not criticize the family's choices. He refused to believe the stereotype that families like Carmen's, who make choices different from what other families or teachers would make, "don't care" about their child's education. Because Carmen's parents saw that their values were being respected, they felt safe to rethink their choice. Without a positive relationship, her teacher and family couldn't help each other meet Carmen's needs.

Teachers who ignore a child's home culture or a family's values and priorities create obstacles to the family feeling they can be themselves *and* be part of the classroom community. But for teachers to become aware of a family's culture can take effort, since its values and influences are not always easily visible in the classroom setting. Cultures differ about expressing feelings, touching, who speaks first to whom, eye contact, how far away adults may stand from each other, and even the role a teacher should play in a child's life. Behavior that seems unconventional might be exactly what a child is taught at home. Effective teachers seek out parents and learn about their culture, values, needs, expectations, and hopes for their child.

A relationship that is "reciprocal" also means that families have responsibilities, too, to help teachers and programs understand the family's culture and expectations. This child's mother, for example, was proactive in getting her child's needs met, and the program responded by making a space for this family to be "different":

> Josephine's preschool application explained that she regularly needed to have mucus suctioned from her airways to be able to breathe. Together, the director and her mother set up a plan to prepare her teachers and the other families.
>
> There were three preliminary meetings. At one, Josephine's mother used a doll to show the other children how and why her daughter's throat had to be suctioned. She explained that Josephine sat in a wheelchair, but could go pretty much everywhere. She loved to laugh and have fun, made funny jokes, and liked hard puzzles. The children asked the best questions; their parents were nervous and the teachers were anxious.
>
> The children quickly adjusted to life with their new friend, and after a few weeks the adults relaxed. Josephine and her family became part of the class community, which had never included anyone with such demanding physical needs before.

As teachers include parents in the classroom community, they should anticipate that not all families will connect in the same way. Some parents, like Carmen's, may be most comfortable getting to know teachers only at drop-off and pickup times. Others may jump right in, as Josephine's mother did. Respecting difference—across all its dimensions—is crucial if a program is going to be a psychologically safe community for all. This is true especially for families who belong to groups that traditionally have had less power in the society, or who feel less comfortable in school or group care settings, or whose children stand out in some way.

A program ensures a more inclusive community when it can answer yes to these questions: Are everyone's values accorded respect? Are all children and families included? Are we sure no child or family is being excluded or denied full participation?

Appreciating a teacher's efforts

A teacher nurtures a positive partnership with families when she acknowledges the stress and strong feelings that sending a child off to preschool can trigger, as well as the specialness of the parent-child bond. Families do the same for that teacher when they give her their support. This is especially appreciated during the teacher's first days with their sometimes confident but often distressed children, all adjusting to the separation at the same time.

A parent's sincere compliment, delivered in person, is always welcome. A simple "thanks for helping us through those first few days" makes any teacher smile. A small, personal gift, such as a gift certificate or homemade cookies, can be nice, as long as the program's policies allow the teacher to accept it. Books, special items, or extra supplies donated to the classroom can make a statement of appreciation for the teacher in her professional role.

But parents may be surprised to know how often a teacher holds onto notes that parents write. This note, thanking the teacher for her insight into a child's interests, encouraged her in her efforts:

> "Every member of our family tried the science experiment you sent home with Levi. Best of all, he can't wait to get back to school to tell you about how it worked. I know that for days, Levi has been whining and begging me to take him home when I drop him off, but you certainly figured out how to engage him. Thank you for helping our son become enthusiastic about school."

Another teacher, who worked hard to make family members struggling with English feel comfortable communicating with her, was rewarded with this grateful note from one parent:

> "Fer the Teacher—I not good at writin English but I want tel you my boy happy wit you. Wen you sended pictur to my boy he want to see you in skol. Bless you and I say praers fer you when I go to church."

A note that honors a teacher's success is always gratifying:

> "After those first tumultuous days and all those stomachaches, I was worried. But now I know that the educational and developmental bricks you have laid this year will be a firm foundation in Deborah's future. I am also happy to tell you that the stomach pains that Deborah had every day in September are completely gone."

9

Closure and Moving On

The lament, "I loved school; I don't want it to be over!" from a child who wept at the classroom door on her first day highlights the importance of sensitively bringing a current experience to a close. Separation is an ongoing, lifelong process, not a single event. The transitions into preschool, back home each day, and eventually from one classroom, program, or grade to the next are all a part. Young children need the understanding and support of their teachers and families during all of them.

Ending the experience with ritual

Our goal in matters of attachment and separation is to make children feel safe in exploring the world and to foster in them a sense of confidence, self-worth, and autonomy. The end of an experience, then, should not be regarded as a time of loss. Rather, children's families and teachers should design opportunities to revisit children's growth individually and in the preschool community.

Here's one teacher's account of her preschool's ritual. It is easily adaptable for most children 4 and older, offering as many variations and technological possibilities as there are programs across the country:

> "Shortly before the end of school, our teachers or willing parents invite children, one or two at a time, to walk through the school and collect physical objects that have been important to them during their time here. One child might choose a tricycle from the outside area, a hat from the dress-up corner, her favorite word game, and a really hard puzzle. Another might choose his friend, the class guinea pig, a favorite cushion, and six beloved books.
>
> "In a space we set up as a photographic studio, the children, one at a time, arrange and rearrange themselves with their chosen objects until they get them the way they want them. Then we photograph them. One child 'collected' his very first teacher, because she held him when he felt scared, he said. He wanted her in his final picture when he was laughing, because he was 'so happy now.'"

The child can make the photographs into a book or save them on CD to share with classmates, visitors, or parents later. If a video camera is available, children can also be recorded talking about why they chose each item. They can talk about how it felt when they first came, what they have learned, who their friends are.

> "For our children this is not casual exploration but a serious retrospective, which they approach thoughtfully. For example, once a child came back after he had photographed his collection, having thought about it overnight. Hassan asked if he could change the books he had chosen. And Joy brought back in two of her paintings that she had at home, so they could be part of her photo. Children value the opportunity to collect and display what mattered most to them in their program."

Resisting the impulse to "grow down"

If we have been successful in providing a safe environment where parents watched their children blossom, parents, too, feel a tug at their hearts as they contemplate leaving. Those early separation struggles in the current setting a fading memory, and the next separation challenge looming, parents may want to cling to the level of ease they and their children have reached. Tanya's mother may well have feelings not so different from her 4-year-old daughter's:

> "I don't want to grow up. I want to grow *down*, and stay right here."

From Tanya's vantage point, why change settings when she's so comfortable?

Although emotionally her mother may agree, resisting the temptation to hang back supports Tanya's development. As the time of the next separation transition approaches, sometimes Tanya might complain or be sad, sometimes she might be firm, insistent, even defiant. What she needs is to hear both parents and teachers say, with resolve and more than once, something like,

> "You are going to have a fifth birthday party very soon. The preschool has room for all the 4-year-olds, but not 5-year-olds. Five-year-olds go to kindergarten in the big school."

When adults do this, it shows we regard the coming transition as a positive step in growing up, without denying that children can feel sad about leaving and happy about starting something new at the same time.

Teachers are human; they can't possibly maintain all the attachments they form with children over the years. A teacher shouldn't carry on with children about how much they will be missed; instead she should show children how much they have accomplished developmentally. Saying, "I can't believe you kids are big enough to leave me" can convey that message.

One teacher who works with children with profound special needs has developed a beautiful tradition to help children get through this latest separation and on to their next challenge. In June, she writes a letter to each one, describing what she thinks that child might be like in 20 years. In every child she finds a little talent, a spark, a clue—nothing unrealistic. For example, she might write,

> "I know you'll be making your own Christmas cards because of the way you did art projects in this class. Everybody who loves you will treasure the cards you send every year."

Parents weep over these letters, filing them away to share later with their child—if or when the child is able to understand.

Every teacher can find a way to end the experience and send children along to the next with something to carry with them. Notice that what this teacher chooses to write belongs to the child, not to her. She doesn't write, "I'll always remember the day you climbed in my lap…"

As in all we do for and with young children, we are working not for close symbiotic relationships but for each child's self-esteem. The best thing we can give them is not our sentiment—the best thing we can give young children is a sense of themselves.

Bibliography

Baker, A.C., & L.A. Manfredi/Petitt. 2004. *Relationships, the heart of quality care: Creating community among adults in early care settings.* Washington, DC: NAEYC.

Balaban, N. 2006. *Everyday goodbyes: Starting school and early care—A guide to the separation process.* New York: Teachers College Press.

Bernstein, J. 1993. *Books to help children cope with separation and loss.* 4th ed. New York: R.R. Bowker.

Bowlby, J. 1969. *Attachment and loss. Volume I: Attachment.* New York: Basic Books.

Bowlby, J. 1973. *Attachment and loss. Volume II: Separation: Anxiety and Anger.* New York: Basic Books.

Eliot, L. 2000. *What's going on in there? How the brain and mind develop in the first five years.* New York: Bantam.

Harwood, R., & J.G. Miller. 1991. Perceptions of attachment behavior: A comparison of Anglo and Puerto Rican mothers. *Merrill-Palmer Quarterly* 37 (4): 583–99.

Honig, A.S. 1993. Mental health for babies: What do theory and research teach us? *Young Children* 48 (3): 69–76.

Honig, A.S. 2002. *Secure relationships: Nurturing infant/toddler attachment in early care settings.* Washington, DC: NAEYC.

Howes, C., & S. Ritchie. 2002. *A matter of trust: Connecting teachers and learners in the early childhood classroom.* New York: Teachers College Press.

Hyson, M. 2004. *The emotional development of young children: Building an emotion-centered curriculum.* 2d ed. New York: Teachers College Press.

Miller, K. 2005. *Simple transitions for infants and toddlers.* Beltsville, MD: Gryphon House.

NAEYC. 2009. Developmentally appropriate practice in early childhood programs serving children from birth through age 8. Position Statement. In *Developmentally appropriate practice in early childhood programs serving children from birth through age*, 3d ed., eds. C. Copple & S. Bredekamp, 1–31. Washington, DC: Author.

Polland, B.K. 2000. *No directions on the package: Questions and answers for parents with children from birth to age 12.* Berkeley, CA: Celestial Arts.

Resch, R. 1977. On separating as a developmental phenomenon: A natural study. *Psychoanalytic Contemporary Science* 5: 197–269.

Szamreta, J.M. 2003. Peekaboo power: To ease separation and build secure relationships. *Young Children* 58 (1): 88–94.

Siegel, D.J., & M. Hartzell. 2003. *Parenting from the inside out: How a deeper self-understanding can help you raise children who thrive.* New York: Jeremy P. Tarcher, Putnam.

Viorst, J. 1998. *Necessary losses: The love, illusions, dependencies, and impossible expectations that all of us have to give up in order to grow.* New York: Free Press.

Warren, R. 1977. *Caring: Supporting children's growth.* Washington, DC: NAEYC.

Children's books

Appelt, K. *Oh my baby, little one*
  This poem follows a baby bird as his mother drops him off at school.
  Although both mother and child are sad when saying good bye, they know
  that they will see each other again soon.

Ballard, R. *My day, your day*
  This book follows children and their parents, showing the sometimes
  surprising parallels between a day at preschool and a day at work. Features
  engaging illustrations of diverse families.

Brown, M.W. *The runaway bunny*
  A little bunny imagines running away from his mother, but she finds him
  every time. Suitable for toddlers.

Cohen, M. *Will I have a friend?*
  Even his father's gentle reassurance doesn't make Jim feel any better. The
  other children in kindergarten are scary strangers to him. He's sure that he'll
  never find a friend … until naptime, when he discovers someone who feels
  the way he does.

Eastman, P.D. *Are you my mother?*
  A bird hatches when its mother is away, so the bird sets out to find her. Its
  efforts pay off when the two are reunited.

Edwards, B. *My first day at nursery school*
  A little girl gets ready for her first day at preschool. But when her mother
  drops her off she protests, "I want my mommy." But she enjoys the wide
  variety of activities, and when her mother arrives she pouts, "I don't want to
  go home, I want to stay at nursery school!"

Janovitz, M. *We love school*
  Happy kittens participate in all of the early childhood activities at school.

Ovenell-Carter, J. *Adam's daycare*
  This book follows Adam's day, starting with a good-bye as his mother drops him off at his family child care center, and ending with him happily returning to his mother at the end of a fun day.

Rey, M., & H.A. Rey. *Curious George's first day of school*
  George is excited that he was invited to be the teacher's helper. He helps with all of the activities, makes a mess with the paints, helps clean up, and is happy that the teacher and the racially diverse group of new friends invite him to come back.

Rusackas, F. *I love you all day long*
  Owen, a little pig, realizes his mommy won't be with him at school so he doesn't want to go. His mother goes over all of the activities and the fact that she will love him while he's doing each of them. She helps Owen to understand that she loves him when they are together and when they are apart.

Sederman, M., & S. Epstein. *The magic box: When parents can't be there to tuck you in*
  Casey's father has to go away for a few days. But he leaves a special box for Casey, so he won't feel so far away. Includes a note to parents.

Senderak, C.H. *Mommy in my pocket*
  Knowing she will miss her mommy when she goes to school, this little bunny imagines shrinking mommy and taking her along in her pocket.

Spelman, C.M. *When I miss you*
  This story uses simple, clear language to express a child's upset feelings about missing a parent and suggests numerous ways to cope.

Sturges, P. *I love school*
  A racially diverse group of children are clearly enjoying all of the activities in a typical preschool day.

Tompert, A. *Will you come back for me?*
  Four-year-old Suki doesn't like the idea of starting preschool until she realizes that her parents will always come back for her at the end of the day.

Weeks, S. *My somebody special*
  In a preschool full of different animals, a little dog is the last to be picked up. As the puppy waits anxiously, the mother rushes from the bus stop to comfort him.

Wilson, K. *Mama always comes home*
  Animal mothers must leave to get food, but they always come back.

Zalben, J.B. *Don't go!*
  A little elephant doesn't want his mother to leave him at preschool. But after she lets him express his feelings and reassures him that she will come back, he has a great day.

Early years are learning years

Become a member of NAEYC, and help make them count!

Just as you help young children learn and grow, the National Association for the Education of Young Children—your professional organization—supports you in the work you love. NAEYC is the world's largest early childhood education organization, with a national network of local, state, and regional Affiliates. We are more than 100,000 members working together to bring high-quality early learning opportunities to all children from birth through age eight.

Since 1926, NAEYC has provided educational services and resources for people working with children, including:

• *Young Children*, the award-winning journal (six issues a year) for early childhood educators

• **Books, posters, brochures, and videos** to support your work with young children and families

• **The NAEYC Annual Conference**, which brings tens of thousands of people together from across the country and around the world to share their expertise and ideas on the education of young children

• **Insurance plans** for members and programs

• **A voluntary accreditation system** to help programs reach national standards for high-quality early childhood education

• **Young Children International** to promote global communication and information exchanges

• **www.naeyc.org**—a dynamic Web site with up-to-date information on all of our services and resources

To join NAEYC

To find a complete list of membership benefits and options or to join NAEYC online, visit **www.naeyc.org/membership**. Or you can mail this form to us.
(Membership must be for an individual, not a center or school.)

Name _____

Address_____

City_____ State_____ ZIP _____

E-mail_____

Phone (H)_____ (W) _____

❏ New member ❏ Renewal ID #_____

Affiliate name/number _____

To determine your dues, you must visit **www.naeyc.org/membership** or call 800-424-2460, ext. 2002.
Indicate your payment option

❏ VISA ❏ MasterCard ❏ AmEx ❏ Discover

Card #_____Exp. date _____

Cardholder's name _____

Signature_____

Note: By joining NAEYC you also become a member of your state and local Affiliates.

Send this form and payment to
NAEYC, PO Box 97156, Washington, DC 20090-7156

LINCOLN CHRISTIAN UNIVERSITY

123187